YOU WILL KNOW WHEN YOU GET THERE

Allen Curnow

# YOU WILL KNOW
# WHEN YOU GET THERE

*poems 1979–81*

AUCKLAND UNIVERSITY PRESS

OXFORD UNIVERSITY PRESS

*The publishers acknowledge assistance from
the New Zealand Literary Fund*

*To C. K. Stead*

## ACKNOWLEDGMENTS

My thanks are due to the editors of *Encounter, Islands, London Magazine,* and *PN Review,* in which most of these poems first appeared.

For 'A Fellow Being' I have helped myself to detail from Dick Scott's account of F. J. Rayner (*Fire on the Clay,* Auckland 1979) which also refreshed a memory of remarks by Aucklanders of an older generation. Of course, the historian is not answerable for the poet's conceptions. My uses of Eliot R. Davis's memoir (*A Link with the Past,* 1948) are, I think, self-explanatory.

*A.C.*

# CONTENTS

The world can end any time
it likes, say, 10.50 am
of a bright winter Saturday,

that's when the *Bay Belle*
casts off, the diesels are picking
up step, the boatmaster leans

to the wheel, the white water
shoves Paihia jetty back.
Nobody aboard but the two of us.

Fifteen minutes to Russell
was once upon a time
before, say, 10.50 am.

The ketch slogging seaward
off Kororàreka Point,
the ensign arrested in

mid-flap, are printed and
pinned on a wall at the end
of the world. No lunch

over there either, the place
at the beach is closed. The *Bay
Belle* is painted bright

blue from stem to stern.
She lifts attentively. That
will be all, I suppose.

## A TOUCH OF THE HAND

Look down the slope of the pavement
a couple of kilometres, to where it empties
its eyeful of the phantoms of passers-by

into mid-morning light which tops it up again
with downtown shadows. There has to be a city
down there and there is, and an 'arm of the sea',

a cloud to sprinkle the pavement, a wind
to toss your hair, otherwise your free hand
wouldn't brush it from your eyes, a welcome

touch of sincerity. As they pass down hill
away from you, their backs, and uphill towards you
their faces, the ages, the sexes, the ways

they are dressed, even one 'smile of recognition',
beg an assurance the malice of your mind
withholds. Look down, confess it's you or they:

so empty your eye and fill it again, with
the light, the shadow, the cloud, the other city,
the innocence of this being that it's the malice

of your mind must be the ingredient making
you possible, and the touch which brushes
the hair from your eyes on the slope of the pavement.

It becomes 'unnaturally' calm
the moment you wonder who's going
to be first to ask what's happened
to the wind when did we last see

or watch for it animate the
bunched long-bladed heads
of the *ti* tree and all the dials
fidget in the sky and then it did

and we breathed again? The moment
comes when the bay at the bottom
of the street has been glassy a moment
too long the wind is in a bag

with drowned kittens god knows
when that was and which of us
will be first to say funny what's happened?
And it won't be a silly question

when it's your turn in the usual
chair to stare up into the cloud-cover
in which a single gull steeply
stalling dead-centred the hole

in a zero the stillest abeyance
and vanished into the morning's
expressionless waterface
'not a line on paper' your finger

pricks as if it might but won't
be lifted for something say switch
off the 'life support system' of the
whole damned visible material

world quite calmly would that be
fair to the neighbours or the birds
other ideas? Seven stilts
at a standstill a study in black

and red beaks all the better to
stab with are modelling for Audubon
mounted on sand in the frame of your
own choice with nothing to shift

the cloud around the morning could
easily be dead mirror to mouth
not the foggiest hope fluttering
the wind-surfer lies flat on the beach

failing actual wind a pressure from
that quarter north-east as it happens
and another pressure like time
squeezes the isthmus the world you

didn't switch off so that coolly
as you recline bare-armed looking
up the spongy firmament has begun
drizzling the paper's getting wet

put the pen down go indoors
the wind bloweth as it listeth or listeth
not there's evidently something
up there and the thing is the spirit

whistle for it wait for it
one moment the one that's one too
many is the glassiest calm an
'intimate question' for the asking.

One more of those perfections
of still water with houses
growing like trees with trees dipped
in first light
           that pearl of a
cloud excited by sunrise
may or may not be priceless
fine weather is not what it
was and you pay more every
day yesterday's blue was of
a depth and a brilliance you
don't find now
                rich eccentric
having wisely ingested
his cake has it too dying
among treasures the weather
troubles him very little
you too Ananias keep
back part of the price
                    it all
hangs by a breath from the south
you too pushing seventy
wishing the weather were here

to stay the morning's moment
free
    knowing that it is not.

A FELLOW BEING

I
How is it that the thought
occurs
          over again of not
being (myself that is being
not) Dr Rayner
                    and that when
it does that same moment the thought
of being him
                he being
dead for one thing and in
the light of such darkness
a fellow being?
                    The syllogism
bubbles like
                    a fart in a bottle
all men (major term) are
mortal all
                doctors (minor term)
are men
            therefore all
doctors
            divinity dentistry
laws letters sciences cats

18

horses Dr Faustus Dr
Syntax Dr Slop and Thomas
the angelic Dr are
                    (were)
mortal alas
            there's a stone
with four names on it press
clippings photographs the year was
1931
        therefore
as things stand in the 'poetry
of fact' he's dead enough and I'm
alive (enough)
                    the sillyolgism
says that makes two of us and
what are we going to do about
that
        *sub specie*
*aeternitatis*?
            Anyway the
thought occurs and it's a fact
'attested by'
                the occurrence from
time
        to time.

19

## II

A yellowing sunrise
heightens the cliff
deepens the sea
                    the
wink of a lizard's
eye ago
        that's eighty
years
        and we're young
and getting rich isn't
the answer we want
to get big
            'a big fish'
already the American
Dental Parlors with
46,000 pleased patients
nothing to the money
he married
                more of that
later
        what else did
the sun that comforts my
westward windows
offer
        to his gaze and
grasp?
            I've a use for
this valley
                the same one
what else did he 'see by the

'dawn's early light'?
a rare and a dreadful
vegetation
           vast bole by
swollen bole
               a sickness
peculiar to the soil
of the island stuffed up
into the sky jamming the
exits to the world
valley and belly
tumoured
           a case of
gigantism
               (pathological)
bole by bole sheer as
Karnak
        oh skip it
*said the old priest of Ammon*
what's holy about Karekare
sheer's sheer in Egypt
we know our geometry
moon-rockets are bigger and
dildoes are smaller
refinery chimneys
aren't trees
               (repeat trees)
Dr Rayner looked north
with an eye to the uses of
surgery and the cost
of extraction

                    measuring
the height of the ridge
                            made it
1000 feet and too
steep for a tramway but
by God I'll
            *Timber!*
*We've come and we'll stay till*
*there's not a stick standing.*


                    III
Agathis australis a lofty
massive
            massive! tree
100 ft. (30 m.) high
sometimes far
higher with columnar
                        columnar!
trunk 3 – 10ft. diam.
or even more
                more!
spreading head of great
branches geysers pumping
cloudy jets clouds forming
dissipating
            sap is rivers
pouring the wrong way
up
    up!


                    22

always on the
boil fruit a hard ovoid or
globose cone which falls to
pieces
          when ripe scattering
compressed winged
                        winged!
seeds
      a forest a throw
where the March sun thrust
and thudded among the great
branches
            till they came
and out there the sea's
full of fish and the myths all
dry on the beach


                    IV
and this god guy
                  see
cuts the dad god's balls off
be-cause the mum god
                        see
gets mad the way he kicks these
kids around
                see and
all this blood'n spunk sloshed like
she been blocked by these guys
they reckon was gods

23

                        see
and she's preg again this other
bunch of kids giants
                        they reckon
and he chucked his dad's balls
in the sea and that's how this other
chick got born that's what wet
dreams is about
                all balls and
bloody great lumps of fat
wodya reckon
                        a rust-pimpled
car clatters down the valley
surfboards lashed tight
                                the boys
balance beautifully
                        half-erect
riding the boards arabesquing
green bellies translucencies
another wave rides fills bursts
pours upward
                dry on the beach
a 'mature female' reads the
Woman's Weekly snuggling
bare breasts in warm sand
scallop and *tuatua* shells
lie around
                unoccupied.

## V

The soul of F. J. Rayner incarnated
in Toronto graduated doctor
of dental surgery Chicago

and there one-fleshed a
meat-packer's heiress happy couple
'holidaying in Delaware Park N.Y.'

top-hat and redingote side by side
in a motorised sulky of thé
period c. 1897 thereafter 'toured

'the world' not excluding Auckland
New Zealand where the above
mentioned stone bears also and

only the names of 'his friends'
2 Moodabes 1 Cole 'remembering his
'sterling qualities and great

'kindness' the soul of the doctor
sits at his study desk it
wears a starched Edwardian collar

cuffs necktie and pin it is
looking straight at me with a look
of an expression arrested yes

'a straight face' generally speaking
success doesn't smile the soul
of the doctor is no exception

its hair parted a little to the side
its moustache is a seal's the right
hand closed not clenched the left

rested on the desk shows one
big ring its trousers are confident of
'covering the loins and legs'

a well-tailored imagination
is the mufti of the soul
of the doctor behind his left

shoulder the barque *Njord* loading
timber an antique telephone
squats at his elbow

Rayner speaking *Doctor* Rayner
long-distance to Wellington
the threaded voices

looping around lakes volcanoes
you can tell the Minister
he can cut it up for butcher's blocks

or toothpicks for all I care
that's my price for the finest
*kauri* in the colony I can ship it

to Sydney or Manila or the moon
for double the money the money
talking the soul's language

which sits as if spiked
upright on crossed buttocks
reminded that there's a pain

commoner and more mortal than
the toothache and a chair
perfectly designed for the purpose

of holding the soul in an erect
position the way they will say
'the eyes follow you' and why

do the eyes do so? You can't
flap them off like flies you've
got to do better than that.


VI

Other ways of putting the same
thing an abstraction a sum
of money
        big deal


*£1,000 Reward*
for any dentist practicing in Auckland today who
can prove that he is the Originator of Painless
Dentistry. We are Auckland's best and largest
dental Concern. ELECTRICITY USED IN
ALL DEPARTMENTS.
      ODONTUNDER
makes pulling and filling painless. We have pur-
chased the secret of its manufacture . . . we pull
more teeth positively painless than all other

whom Eliot R. Davis nonpareil
colonial brewer hotelier racing
man high-class pig breeder could
'only say' he found

a most genial man and the cheeriest of company
at all times. A dentist by profession and an
extremely clever businessman with an immense
number of commercial interests. He had a huge
forest of kauri timber on the West Coast near the
Manukau Harbour, out of which he made a small
fortune.

mile after mile precipitously
rifted ranges the cliff-bottom
beaches Whatipu Karekare
Paratohi Rock waist deep offshore
Piha Anawhata
　　　　　　　having told his
nephew/secretary Prouting who
told Dick Scott (historian) 20
years was too long to wait in a
pond the size of the U.S.A.
to become a big fish in a pond

28

like New Zealand I could be big
right away if anything bothered me
I could just eat it
                    an abstraction
one thing becoming another
'kind of poem' not leaving the
thing intact
                    all those trees and
Ethel his wife a lyric in her own
right 'a very wealthy woman' having
'a financial interest in Universal
'Pictures Hollywood' the movies
hit Queen Street
                    an abstraction registered
as the Hippodrome Picture Company
and plenty more
                    'a splendid cook'
in the opinion of Eliot R.
recollecting Moose Lodge later Cole's
where the Queen slept
                    long after
and the doctor's well-equipped launch
*The Moose* for trolling the lapping lake
waters of Rotoiti
                    'the finest
'grilled trout imaginable'
                    Ethel
whose money 'it was generally felt
'he was turning to good account'
travelled much of the time in Europe and
the U.S.

                    life being practical criticism
of the poetry of wealth
                            is unspoiled
Nature any use after all and
what are we doing here?
                                'unfortunately
'in very bad health' she died
in Canada having left this country
not long before
                        date omitted.




                VII
Late among the locusts
to the ripest crop
'columnar' Karekare
valleys to the north
late among the locusts
the saw-teeth shining
for the swollen centuries
the locusts hadn't yet
eaten
        seven years
a few million board-feet
later and the big seas
which skittled the beach
tramway one wild
king tide and the bank paid the
doctor what he said
he sold that mill to


                30

the Government
               having
the right friends clearing
£18,000
and £100,000
royalties the sterling
quality of the man
and
      why don't you send
the money to America
Fred? they said
Kaiser Bill's at the gates
of Paris anything can
happen
            no it can't
God won't let it and
built himself a statelier
mansion in Almorah
road Epsom Auckland
'magnificent view of the
'harbour and landscape'
and there was *talk*
                  doesn't he
know there's a war on?
what about those flashing lights
from the windows pro-German
don't tell me von Luckner's
not watching
                  prisoner of Motuihe
island
      and why's he got that

Turkish bath with mirrors
all round and the *electric*
lights under the mirrors and the
doors between the bedrooms
hidden in the wardrobes?


VIII

'lots of detractors the usual lot
'of men who make good financially
'or any other way' so Eliot R.

whose mum-in-law (1911) bought the
first Rolls Royce seen in New Zealand
and who motored one day with the doctor

to Hamilton a hundred miles to the
music of boiling radiators
and exploding 'pneumatic' tyres

and who (Eliot R. that is) did
know there was a war on and sailed
to Sydney twice one month 'buying and

'selling whisky in big quantities'
on which active service having been lucky
not to die pondered the all-wisdom of

the One who 'shapes our ends' ordaining
the *Wimmera* (poor Captain Kell)
must hit a mine and not the *Manuka*

preciously freighted with 'another batch
'of whisky from the Americans' Charlie Macindoe
and not least if last Eliot R.

who lived 30 years more to put on record
appreciatively that the doctor 'a great
'Bohemian always lived on the best'.


IX

The fatty fumes of Abels
margarine factory 'wafted'
on the north-easterly weather
heavy and warm this autumn
creep under low cloud-cover

up the affluently wooded
elevations of Almorah Road
the young executives and the
professional men understand
glossy pictures don't stink

the doctor's uplifted house
or home if that's the idea
is intact a stately shanty
by a World War I domestic
architect out of *Country Life*

in Hampstead it would've had more
knobs but if any fool's folly
ran to hallways two floors high

33

30ft long the wainscoting
wouldn't be Karekare *kauri*

stained rosewood colour or
the upper floors cladded
with weathering cedar shingles
and the shallow-pitched roof
so anxiously angled an

architecture of evasions
and asseverations *le style*
*c'est l'homme* Sir Carrick
Robertson 'prominent surgeon'
afterwards liked the outlook

over the trees the unedited
harbour views anybody's islands
a 'beautifully situated'
shabbiness too has its own
classical attributes

grubbiness its grandeurs under
the doctor's porte cochère
the latest cheesiest-lacquered
Japanese hatchback snuggles
long after half of the gardens

and the croquet lawn sliced
off in a storm of steel
pitched from the edge into the age
and the gorge of the motorway leaving
a house with nowhere to fall.

X

I might remember the year you
died but not for that reason
paths cross where nobody comes or
somebody's late it must have

been that in 1931
your soul could have dragged itself
as far as the dawn clifftop
over Anawhata or been torn

from death duties or been sucked
up and scaled off with the sea fog
or spilled into the creeks which drain
the steepnesses worming

its way the dragonflies and
the mosquitoes rise in their day
on wings of success humming
the way money hums and the saw-teeth

your life-cycle and mine
humming the hymn of it's finished
to the tune of it's just begun
fifty years 'later' the

questions open as the high-pitched
morning gapes to the sea
what was all the hurry? and who
on earth is that leaning into the

freshening westerly? *Agathis
australis* could've towered and
rotted in peace any number
of irrelevant centuries the year

I remember is the first I visited
the sun-drowning clifftop and
you died the two facts being
unconnected except I've come

where the paths cross the two of us
on collusion course the
'columnar' the elephant-limbed
conifers of this western

ocean toppled and rolled you
had only to lift your hand the
dank valleys delivered
shiploads ships houses theatres

railway cars the seeds are flying
down into the teeth of the wind
the bulldozers the week-end visitors
in March on my roof the bursting

cone wakes me like hail the soul
flies this way and that in the thinning
dawn dark where the paths cross and the
young trees know only how to grow.

AFTER DINNER
*Arnold Wall 1869–1966*


At ninety he told the press,
I suppose you are going to ask me
how I manage to live so long,
and so well.
                    Five years later,
facing me across his table,
having lifted the glass of red
wine to an untremulous
lip, and set it down
with a steady hand, he remarked
that he once possessed the whole
of the *Comédie Humaine*
in a Paris edition. Couldn't
remember now what became of it.

Between him and his death's
left foot the gangrene was
no secret, already in the door
and pressing hard, in a white fold freshly
dressed for dinner.
                    Other whitenesses
were summits, mountain faces,
alps both Southern and Swiss,

Tibet, one icy toehold
after another, still climbing now
in the thinnest air, the last
of all those ups and downs.

Having read many books, taught some,
and written a few, after dinner
announced, as it were, a decision,
I have been here long enough.

A little after that, Lawrence?
D. H. Lawrence? Terrible young man.
Ran away with my friend Weekley's wife.

All true, as it happened. Twice
the mortifying foot, from under the table
published his pang, the grimace no sooner
read than cancelled, very civilly.

Absently the proof-reader corrects
the typesetter. According to copy
the word is exotic. He cancels
the literal r and writes an x.

A word replaces a word. Discrepant
signs, absurd similitudes
touch one another, couple promiscuously.
He doesn't need Schopenhauer

to tell him only exceptional intellects
at exceptional moments ever get any
nearer than that, and when they do
it gives them one hell of a fright.

He's exercised, minding his exes and ars.
If Eros laughs, as the other philosopher
says, and if either word's a world
'offering plentiful material for humour',

that's not in copy. After dark,
that's when the fun starts, there's a room
thick with globes, testers, bell-pulls
rare fruits, painted and woven pictures,

*pakeha* thistles in the wrong forest,
at Palermo the palm lily *ti australis*
in the Botanical Gardens, Vincento
in white shorts trimming the red canoe

pulled the octopus inside out
like a sock, *Calamari!* The tall German
blonde wading beside, pudenda awash,
exquisitely shocked by a man's hands

doing so much so quickly,
*Calamari!* Those 'crystalline'
aeolian shallows lap the anemone
which puckers the bikini, her delicacy.

Short of an exceptional moment, if only
just! In his make-do world a word
replaces a white vapour, the sky
heightens by a stroke of the pen.

The feathers and the colours cry
on a high note which ricochets
off the monologue of the morning sun
the long winded sea, off Paratohi posturing
on a scene waiting to be painted.

Scarlet is a squawk, the green
yelps, yellow is the tightest cord
near snapping, the one high note, a sweet-sour
music not for listening. The end is
less than a step and a wink

away as the parakeet flies.
Darkness and a kind of silence under
the cliff cuts the performance,
a moment's mixture. Can scavenging
memory help itself?

What do I imagine coloured words
are for, and simple grammatical
realities like, 'I am walking to the beach'
and 'I have no idea what the sky can mean
'by a twist of windy cloud'?

What's the distance between us all
as the rosella cries its tricolour
ricochet, the tacit cliff, Paratohi
Rock in bullbacked seas, my walking eye
and a twist of windy cloud?

I

High and heavy seas all the winter
dropped the floor of the beach the whole mile
exposing more rocks than anybody
imagined the biggest surprise a
reef the size of a visiting beast
you have to walk round
                              a formation
out of the gut of the gales the noise
the haze the vocabulary of
water and wind
                    the thing 'demands an
'answer'
              I know you do you know me?


the sea shovels away all that loose
land and shovels it back underfoot's
a ball of sand stitched together with
spun lupin and looping spinifex
making it look natural
                              little
as you like to think nothing's either
covered or uncovered for ever.

A wall of human bone the size
of a small church isn't easy
to conceive
                 neither is the rock
which overhangs me overhung
itself by cloud-cover cupping
the uproars of up-ended seas
and overhanging us all the
hot star which nothing overhangs


the wig it wears is trees knotted
by the prevailing westerlies
'chapleted' with clematis and
kowhai at this height of the spring's
infestations of white and gold
a cerebrum behind the bone
'thinking big'
                      proportionately
to the size of the thing
                            doesn't
have to be visible if it
stoops to speak so to speak the word
of a stony secret dislodged
the creator knows he's made it!
his mate matter
                     out of nothing
a tied tongue loosed the stony ghost
before all of us talking all
at once in our own languages
the parakeet's brilliant remarks

the fluent silences of the
eel in the pool
                    I think the rock
thinks and my thought is what it thinks.


III

A rock face is creased in
places in others cracked
through to itself I have

never climbed though children
sometimes do up to the
chin of the cave below

I always look up though
something else is always
uppermost a cloud scuds

past the sun reappears
yellow lichens ashy
patches thicken sicken

on the skin of the face
of the rock from spots the
size of the iris of a

mouse's eye to a smashed
egg the rock is wetted
by a weeping lesion

45

long after the rain stopped
it looks down I look up
a wink is sufficient.


IV

Memory is a stonier
place at the farm they called it
Rocky Gully blackberry
claws me back where I'm crawling

pistol-gripping the rifle
at arm's length after the hurt
hare my two bullets in its
body and couldn't reach it

where the third aimed blindly hit
home recesses of mother
rock overhang me and the
sun the rock offering no

choice of exit under the
one skin hare and hound I catch
myself listening for the shot
in the dark I shall not hear.

Brasch wrote 'these islands' and I
'two islands' counting one short,
and 'the islands' in our language
were remoter, palmier Polynesian chartings,
a there for a here.
                        The cartographer
dots them in, the depth of his blue
denotes the depth of the entirely
surrounding water.
                        The natives,
given time, with the help of an atlas,
come to recognize in the features of
the coastline a face
of their own, a puzzled mirror
for a puzzling globe.
                            'Always in these
'islands', that was Charles Brasch
getting it right the very first time.

Pat Laking knew it by heart the whole sonnet
all the way down to 'distance
'looks our way' and it did,
over the martinis in Observatory Circle,
Washington D.C., demanding by way

of an answering look nothing more
than an excellent memory.

That was
8 November 1974, just about
midnight, give or take a few minutes.

Hearing my name in the barnsize bar
of the Tokomaru pub where you cross the road
and walk into the Pacific
Rua made me a small
comically deferential bow
spreading his hands as far
apart as they could go
'You are a *haapuka*!'

and I affecting modesty
comically flattered
flatteringly comic with
hands a bit closer together
'No not a *haapuka* a *kahawai*'

and Rua closing his hands
to the little fish size
perfect at this game
'Perhaps a *maomao*?'

a long way off in the city
in another sort of bar
one stuffed rainbow trout adorned
the wall and a mirror swimmingly
reflected the weed and the cloud
a jam jar full of tadpoles.

None of those was Eden.
  I was as far
from that as from this, one's
  own personal
infancy of orchard
  grass grasshoppers
and a Black Prince apple
  or ten summers
later the long breath held
  bursting under-
water in Corsair Bay
  and breaking
surface from the deep green
  dive,
      the breathless
exhalation tweaking
  the neck, half-blind
fish snapping at sunlight.
  None of those was
anywhere near,
          neither was
  the summer come
of sex, give me a hand
  I'll take it.
Fifty onces and sinces,

        paradises
are statistics, I'm as
     far as *ever*,
the older one gets the
     better one gets
the hang of it all the
     *essential*
onceness.
               Visitors dig
other people's Edens,
     there's a sign in
Sicily GROTTA DI
     POLIFEMO,
when you get there you see
     why Homer was
blind as a bat and the
     town football pitch
is netted all round with
     rusty wire.
Interesting,
               the way
     the English say
*round the corner* and the
     Romans *cento*
*metri.*
        I'm a stranger
     here myself,
sorry,
          give me a hand.
     You heard what the
man said, keep right on you
     can't miss it.

## ORGANO AD LIBITUM

*For beauty with her bande*
*These croked cares hath wrought,*
*And shipped me into the lande,*
*From which I first was brought.*
  Thomas, Lord Vaux 1510–1556


I

Time's up you're got up to kill
the lilies and the ferns on wires
the brightwork the sorrowful silk
ribbons the cards the cars

the black twelve-legged beast
rises the dance begins
the six shoulders heave
you up the organist sits

with his back to you and your hobbling
pomp *largo* it says
*e grave* his fingers walk but
none of the feet is in step

he polishes the stool he rocks on
the bones of his arse he reaches
for a handful of stops he's nodding
yes to your proceeding

perched on a mountain with
'rows upon rows of pipes
'set in cliffs and precipices'
growing and growing 'in a blaze

'of brilliant light' that sort
of stuff is packaging
printed matter only if only
there were more to it than that

(shriek!) you could see 'his body
'swaying from side to side amid the
'storm of huge arpeggioed
'harmonies crashing overhead'

in a cloud a bandaging whiteout
'his head buried forward towards
'a keyboard' busier than God
and you that wool-shed sleeper

the one who saw in his dream
was it Handel high among the icefalls the
big wig nodding mountainously
swaying playing the instrument

had to be big enough to drown
Sam Butler's rivers up there in
Erehwon chapter IV and climbed
uselessly towards the source

of the music this isn't a dream
west of the main divide
Nowherehwon sounds no trumpets
this afternoon everyone present is

wide awake nobody's dreaming
least of all you (you) steady there
hang on *taihoa*! the organist's
fingers trot he breathes through

dusty curtains a husky
*vox humana* out of dusty
pipes fat candles for Sister
Cecilia's jig-time fingering

diddledy-dancing you down
hold tight there brother in the box
saying after me 'It was
'no dreme: I lay brode waking' and


II

saying after me it was *raunchy*
and heavy with lilies in the chapel of
Walerian Borowczyk's blue (blue)
nunnery
          she leaned she fondled the
keyboard the pipes blew kisses
to the mouth her virgin sisters
dressed the altar-table dusted
the pews
          every one a beauty
(beauty) 'dangerous; does set danc-
'ing blood' Fr Hopkins S.J.
specialist

          swaying she swept up
nympholept handfuls flung
on the bloodstream a sister playing
*organo ad libitum* jiggetty-jig on the
woodcutter's cock and the butcher's
block
        Paris having the rottenest
summer for years the crowds
packed in out of the rain to the
Cinéma Paramount leaving
Montparnasse to the web-footed tourists
and the taxis
            dead in her bed
by toxic additive smuggled and
slipped from the knickers to the coffee cup
the gaunt Mother lay
              and they danced
their hot pants down on the stony
gallery for joy of their nubility
crying 'La Mère est morte!' they
swung on the bellrope naked making the
bell-mouth boom at the sun
                 one
sneeze of the gusting equinox
whipped the doors from the bolts and up
went the scarlet skirts of the cardinal
dead leaves and fingers
            flying
to the roaring organ the guffaw
of the daylight and the rain pouring
from the outside in

55

                              the movie's
over
        will you get up and go?




                    III
The organist blows his nose folds
his music switches the power off

getting into the 'waiting cars' they
postpone the politics of eternity

till time permits which is after the
cards the flowers the municipal

oil-fired furnace the hole
in the ground one after after

another thereafter before you
know where you are you were.




                    IV
No bookshelf in the room
                        the Gideons'
bible in the drawer the last occupant
never opened is a black book
lying in wait
                lucky you brought


                    56

your bedside paperbacks prismatic
blue green yellow purple
one celebrated psychiatric
teacher and there's this marvellous
meteorite or enormous
boulder of Magritte a motto for
Sisyphus beneath which you are that
prone figure folded in scarlet perfectly
composed exposed in a
window for anyone who cares to know
what it's like in these rooms for sleeping
off life
       'O Faustus lay that
'damned book aside read read
'the scriptures' watch out for the
fish-hooks in the small print


         v

                 mark
the exits fasten your bible-belt
for take-off
        'the unlikely event
'of an emergency'
            he sits with his
back to you 'busier than God' his
instrument flashes the crash is
programmed the music is magnified the
size of the side of an antarctic
volcano

you disintegrate there
*buzz buzz*
　　　　　with or without your
loved ones and a face the mirror has
forgotten.


VI
　　　　　After is a car door
closing
　　　*chlomp*
a blinking light a wide gate
the main road
　　　　　*chlomp*
can I take you anywhere?


VII
Hands on the wheel and eyes on the road
reprieved into the time of day they notice
a yellow bus turning a tired female trundling

groceries 'belief in a hereafter'
wasn't so difficult was it? hardest of all
to believe what actually happens come to think

the difficulty was never to have believed
willingly in heat o'the sun or winter's rages
nor that here after all the hereafter hadn't much

going for it notwithstanding the beauty of
the language nor been listening
when the little dog said you can't eat it and you

can't fuck it sour grapes dogs having no
souls if you believe the books and what's
so special about you in your situation

apropos eating and fucking and
who writes the books? only men who do both or
if no-one did wouldn't exist.


                          VIII
*palingenesis*
                    five syllables' worth
of pure vacation
                          round trip
                               returning
you don't know you've been
                               born twice not again
'Fie upon such errors!
                          To hear stuff of that
'nature rends mine ears'
                          Panurge said but Arthur
(Schopenhauer) three
                          hundred years after
rather liked the thought
                          looked forward to a
hereafter stocked with
                          genuine spare parts

                     59

good as new nothing to
                          burden the memory
naked on the beach
                          now storms from the west
stand the sea on end
                          it's an instrument
big enough to drown
                          accompanies you
all the way down the
                          'cold front' feathering
inland hanging its
                          gauzes uncloses
closes teases you
                          don't see anything
clearly
        *taihoa*!
                    your replacement's on
his way
        you're naked
                          as the fish bottled
'in its element'
                    lifted to the sun
and it's the same wave
                          spirits you away
out to sea while the
                          biodegradable
part picks up its heels
                          recycles all its
degradations
                fresh
                    wreaths every time and
no resurrections.

                    The organist
locks up the console
                    Handel
booms at the sun
                    Tiziano's
rapt airborne virgin in the Frari
was an assumption removed *per*
*restauro* in '74 that too was a day of
sun wind and rain
                    Domenico's
mother said and he quoted 'life
'is bitter we must sweeten the coffee'
shovelling the sugar
                    *chlomp*
'towards the source of the music'
                              *chlomp*
and they made the bell-mouth swing
swinging on the bell-rope
                    naked.

Nobody comes up from the sea as late as this
in the day and the season, and nobody else goes down

the last steep kilometre, wet-metalled where
a shower passed shredding the light which keeps

pouring out of its tank in the sky, through summits,
trees, vapours thickening and thinning. Too

credibly by half celestial, the dammed
reservoir up there keeps emptying while the light lasts

over the sea, where it 'gathers the gold against
it'. The light is bits of crushed rock randomly

glinting underfoot, wetted by the short
shower, and down you go and so in its way does

the sun which gets there first. Boys, two of them,
turn campfirelit faces, a hesitancy to speak

is a hesitancy of the earth rolling back and away
behind this man going down to the sea with a bag

to pick mussels, having an arrangement with the tide,
the ocean to be shallowed three point seven metres,

one hour's light to be left and there's the excrescent
moon sponging off the last of it. A door

slams, a heavy wave, a door, the sea-floor shudders.
Down you go alone, so late, into the surge-black fissure.